OSCAR
The Dog Gone Dog

by "Oscar Mayer" Korver

OSCAR, the dog gone dog

By Bill F. Korver

www.metakoi.com

Copyright 2015 Bill F. Korver. All rights reserved. No portion of this book may be reproduced, stored in a retrieval system, or transmitted in any form or by any other means – electronic, mechanical, photocopy or other- except for brief quotations in printed reviews, without the written consent of the publisher.

Published by Metakoi Publishing and Lightning Source (a subsidiary of Ingram Content Group), 1246 Heil Quaker Boulevard, La Vergne, TN USA 37086

All Scripture quotations, unless otherwise indicated, are taken for the Holy Bible, New American Standard (NAS) version, copyright by the Lockman Foundation.

About the front cover: Pencil drawing by Douglas Rowe. See his work at DouglasRoweStudios.com

Korver, Bill F.

Oscar, the dog gone dog.

ISBN:978-0-9905783-1-4

1. Dogs 2. Korver, Bill 3. Animals

Printed in the United States of America

"A righteous man has regard for

The life of his beast...."

Proverbs 12:10

My name is Oscar. My Dad sometimes calls me Oscar Mayer, after the famous hot dogs, because I once ate twenty-four hot dogs at one time. I'll explain that buffet later. I am a three-year old male, mixed-breed dog (For my paperwork at the veterinarian's office we arbitrarily decided I am half Australian Shepherd and half Golden Retriever! Recently the American Kennel Club officially began calling dogs like me, All-American). I am about twenty inches tall at the shoulder and weigh about fifty-five pounds.

My brief life has been filled with many adventures. This book is about a two month adventure I had recently. Before I tell you about my adventure, let me tell you about myself and my early life. I was born in a shelter, The Safe Haven*, that has a "no kill" policy. No matter how long an animal stays, they do not euthanize any of the dogs or cats. From early on I was different from my litter mates. I had a physical disability. I have a club foot.

My front right leg and paw is bowed and I walk with a bit of a limp. I have a "hitch in my giddy-up", as they say. The veterinarian is not sure if I was born this way or suffered an injury when I was just a small puppy. Either way, I can run very fast,

---

* Not the real name of the shelter

but my walking is a bit out of the ordinary. No doubt, due to living the first fifteen months of my life at a shelter, surrounded by dozens of dogs and cats and with little human interaction, I developed a very skittish nature. Nearly everything will scare me, the smallest noise or the slightest movement. In addition to my personality, my physical condition made me "unadoptable" in the eyes of most people. The Safe Haven would take me and other dogs, as well as cats, to adopt-a-pet events at local pet stores. Hundreds of people would come and be attracted to the cute puppies, but never me. I got to the point where I would just lay in my crate and ignore the people walking by.

One day everything changed! My human mom and her youngest

daughter were at a store that was having an adoption event. The girl had begged for months for a kitten; she had had a puppy before and cats, but never a kitten. The family finally agreed that she could have a kitten. That fateful spring day they came to the store where I, along with many other dogs and cats, was on display. Naturally most people were attracted to the puppies, but not the girl. She was attracted to the "underdog" (pun intended) in me. After a brief family conference, it was agreed – I'd be adopted! I was so frightened the young lady from The Safe Haven had to carry me from the pet store to the family's vehicle in the parking lot. She cried as she carried me…. I have a way of winning peoples' hearts.

Fifteen long months of homelessness were over! The people at The Safe Haven were kind enough, but they only have a few people to volunteer each day. Therefore they can't give much time, attention or affection to all the pets under their care.

My dad says one verse from the Bible, his favorite book, came to his mind when he recalls my adoption. When the ancient nation of Israel chose her first king, Saul, it did so primarily based upon the externals: his looks. He was big, tall and handsome (1 Samuel 9:2). After Saul's miserable run as king, God directed his prophet, Samuel, to anoint the second king, Saul's successor. Samuel almost succumbed to the tendency to look at the external too. He planned to anoint Jesse's oldest son as king due to his appearance. God intervened and directed Samuel to look for another son of Jesse. Jesse had each of his seven older sons pass under the watchful eye of Samuel, but God directed him to the youngest of all the sons. He was such a "long shot" to be anointed as king, his own father had not even brought before the prophet of God, but left him out in the field to tend the sheep! He was, however, the one God chose. While humans tend to look at things that really don't matter, God looks at the heart. That verse that dad loves is, *"But the Lord said to Samuel, 'Do not look at his appearance or at the height of his stature, because I have rejected him* (Jesse's oldest son from being king); *for God sees not as man sees, for man looks at the outward appearance but the Lord looks at the heart"* (1 Samuel 16:7). A song from the 1990's said, "When some men see a shepherd boy, God may see a king". People demonstrate they are taking on God's values when they value people and character more than height, weight, teeth and hair.

When I was first adopted my name was Cody. But since I had little human interaction at the shelter I didn't respond to that name. Due to this fact my new family decided to give me a new name. Dad wanted to name me Mephibosheth, a son of Jonathan, King David's best friend. Mephibosheth was injured in a fall when he was a young boy. We are informed that he was "lame in both feet" (2 Samuel 4:4). Later David showed kindness and grace to this young man by inviting him to eat at the king's table regularly and give him his father's estate and free laborers to work the estate (2 Samuel 9:1-13). It is one of dad's favorite stories in the entire Bible. Mom and Allegra quickly overruled. They said it was far too long a name for them to call out and for me to learn. It didn't just roll off the tongue! My family has an adult son and he suggested my name be Oscar. Oscar it was.... just between you and me, I sure am glad that dad lost that discussion. I don't think I would have ever learned the name Mephibosheth. I would, however, like to eat regularly at the King's table! When you grow up like I did, without normal interaction with people, it can be very hard to let others show you love. Dad says people are a lot like that too. Many have not had the pleasure of a normal family, and when those who love the King try to show them love, they often shy away. Be careful to not think the person who shies away from your kindness, your loving acts, really does not want or need it. It's just that often it's an entirely new experience for them.

I was adopted in April. My family includes my older "sister" Mollie, a purebred Australian Shepherd. Since she's a herder by instinct, she likes to try to herd me around our house and back yard. She likes to fetch things like tennis balls and bring them back to dad, while I just like to run around with no particular aim or direction. Sometimes when we are both running, I run into her and she lets me have it for blindsiding her! Besides having a big sister, Mollie, my family also includes a male Maine Coon cat named Cooper (the younger girl likes the Mini Cooper cars, hence the name). Cooper is about eight years old and weighs about twenty-three pounds, (He's NOT a *Mini* Cooper!). He's the biggest cat I've ever seen, and believe me, I've seen more than my fair share of cats at the shelter!

When I came home with my new family, I had some trouble adjusting to my new home. Mollie and I have a nice fenced yard, but at night dad and mom would put me into a crate, like they had routinely done with Mollie for years. The first two nights I was quiet, but the following nights I was desperate to get out of my "prison cell". After mom read about animals like me who've been adopted, she decided to put me on a blanket on the floor near Mollie in the master bedroom. From that night, I slept like a log and made no sound at all. When I was outside in the yard I had the tendency to hide under azalea bushes in the yard. They would call me and have to come to look under bushes to find me. Slowly I began to get bolder and soon was welcoming my family at the fence when they returned from work or from running errands.

After being with my new family for about three months, they

decided to take an overnight trip a few hours away. Since the weather was forecast to be nice, they provided food and water and a bed as well as a nice big screened in porch with a dog door for me and Mollie to use in case it was too hot or rainy.

The next afternoon when they returned home I was missing! Neither they, nor I, know what possessed me to leave. They think it was mostly due to fear and the anxiety of feeling abandoned. Whatever the reason, I escaped the yard through a small opening where our fence ends and the neighbor's fence begins. After getting out and wandering a bit, I could not find my way home in this new neighborhood! In retrospect, it was the worst decision I have ever made.

Ever notice how life is like that? Rear-view mirror decisions are always easy and good ones. The ones we make in real life are often neither. Perhaps you have heard of the story Jesus told about the lost sheep? If not, He told of a shepherd who had one hundred sheep and when he counted them, there were only ninety-nine, one was lost. It had wandered from his care. Rather than be content that he had the ninety-nine, the shepherd went searching for the lost one. The shepherd left the ninety-nine to search for the one. It was my experience when I was lost that I wished I would have been found. I remembered the soft bed, the good food and the warm fireplace. Problem was, I did not know how to find my way back home and the harder I looked the more lost I became.

If you have a lost sheep in your family, don't give up praying and looking. If you are the lost sheep, please know someone cares and is looking for you! Francis Thompson, a great writer of a past generation, pictured God as the "hound of heaven" He keeps pursuing us, hot on our trail until he tracks us down. If you have ever wondered, He's on your trail…can you sense His presence, His closeness?

What follows is the story of a two month search-and-rescue operation and some of the lessons learned along the way. Most of the details are factual, a few are educated guesses by dad, since I don't have opposable thumbs to hold a pen and didn't think to bring a journal with me when I wandered away, I could not

remember all the details. Dad's done the best he could with the

facts and what we know about animal tendencies and human

nature.

THE EARLY DAYS AND CLOSE CALLS

When I got lost it was a Saturday in June, the day before Father's Day and two days before the youngest girl's eighteenth birthday. My disappearance ruined both celebrations. Dad and mom searched the neighborhood frantically, calling my name and whistling for me. The girl used her computer skills and made flyers with my picture on them to post throughout the subdivision we live in. There are nearly 800 homes in our neighborhood and hundreds more in other neighborhoods nearby. None of the three of them or I slept well that first night.

The second day after my vanishing act, when the flyers were posted in the neighborhood, a lady called dad to inform him she had seen me panting in the 87^0 heat the day before. She said I had lain down under the minivan in her driveway to get out of the direct sunshine. She said she had placed a leash around my neck but when I hesitated to follow her she assumed I could find my way home and let me go. I had been only three blocks from home!

The following day, day three of the saga, a man who works for the local animal control in our county called dad. He had seen the flyer posted in the neighborhood and had spotted me only three blocks from home and was following me in his truck. Dad left work immediately and arrived at the sight in about ten minutes. When he arrived, I was nowhere to be found. The animal control officer stated that a car with a loud exhaust had driven by and frightened me, causing me to run into the woods that border our neighborhood on three sides. Dad, mom and daughter searched the heavily wooded area for quite some time, but saw no dogs, just lots of bugs and thorny vines. They, of course, were saddened by this. The sighting had gotten their hopes up, the loud noise had caused those hopes to be dashed.

The following two days, there were no sightings, no phone calls, nothing. My family was very worried about my hydration. It was late June and the temperature usually is in the 90's and it's very humid in North Carolina. They were praying for my return and safety. God graciously answered those prayers in one sense. The next two days it was several degrees cooler than normal and our area received about a quarter of an inch of rain each day. The weather greatly allayed their fears that I would just die from heat exhaustion. The Bible states a principle often called, by theologians, common grace, "He makes the rain fall on the just and the unjust" (Matthew 5:45). I don't know about your theology, whether you think dogs are just or unjust (I happen to know for a fact that all cats are unjust), but I do know it rained on me those two days! What a nice relief from the heat and it sure made it easy to find a drink from the streams and puddles in the woods.

When I was off on my journey, dad and mom had to remind themselves and were comforted by a truth: God takes notice of the situations animals get themselves into. In the gospel of Matthew, Jesus said, "Look at the birds of the air, that they do not sow, nor reap nor gather into barns, and yet your heavenly Father feeds them…" (Matthew 6:26). In another place, Jesus declared, "Are not two sparrows sold for a cent? And yet not one of them falls to the ground apart from your Father" (Matthew 10:29). I know how much dad and mom paid for me and for my reward and can assure you that it was much more than a penny. God cares for inexpensive birds, lost dogs and I suppose cats too!

Dad started some new routines in an effort to find me. He began getting up earlier than normal and walking the neighborhood or riding his bicycle through the neighborhood, calling my name as he went. Additionally he and mom and youngest daughter would often walk the neighborhood near sunset, when it had cooled down a bit, calling my name as they went. They were hopeful, but hope was ebbing away bit by bit with each passing day.

In our own neighborhood, there was a possible sighting of me about two weeks into my odyssey. I say possible sighting because the people who would call dad and mom could never really be sure if it was me they had seen me if merely another dog that resembled me. When this happened, hope was renewed! My family put a couple of bowls of food and water in two places where these sightings had occurred. The next day one bowl of food and water remained untouched. The other bowl had some of the dog food missing and a note from a nearby neighbor which read, 'PLEASE DO NOT FEED THE CATS!" Dad was not a happy camper, it's probably very good that dad did not know which neighbor wrote the note. He was anxious to find me and did not appreciate having his actions to find me criticized by a petty neighbor who did not know the circumstances behind the food and water.

It is easy to criticize others' actions, especially when you don't know the facts, the particulars, of what they were doing and/or their motives, why they were doing what they were. Before being critical, get the details of what is going on and why. If you don't know the full story, be very slow in passing judgment.

Thankfully, there were far more kind people than mean-spirited people who contacted dad and mom to help. One woman saw dad out looking for me and offered to help. She drove her vehicle around the neighborhood looking for me on at least two occasions. Many others called in response to posters my family had posted in many places and to newspaper advertisements and internet postings. My family met many kind people who were very willing to help them, people they'd never met before, to find a dog they'd never seen.

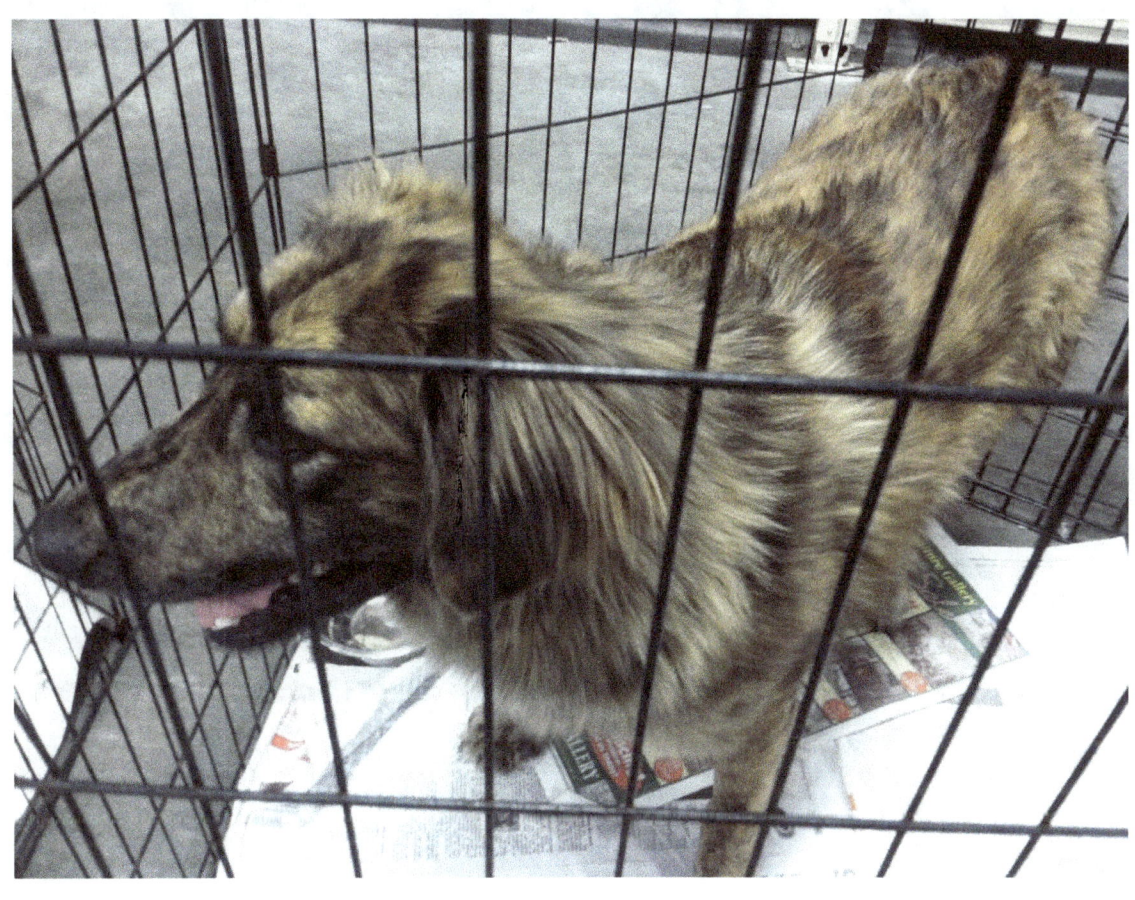

This is me in a crate at the adoption event when mom and Allegra discovered me.

I had a great time exploring my new yard the first week at home!

I had never seen a television before and was fascinated with it. I watched it with Allegra for hours.

Mollie and I don't always get along, because she can be a bossy big sister, but usually we are best friends!

Cooper, Mollie and I love being lazy!

LOST DOG

REWARD IF FOUND

This is a copy of the flyer dad and mom posted all over town when I was lost.

FALSE ALARMS

Perhaps you've gotten excited about something only to have your hopes dashed? That's what happened to dad and mom several times during my season of wandering. They received many tips, usually in the form of phone call, about sightings of me. One week they got about four or five calls from an area about six or seven miles south of our home. The sightings were all in the same general area, one near a local high school, the others near a restaurant and gas station. The sighting near the high school was never confirmed, but as details followed later, it was undoubtedly not me. The restaurant location made some sense, it backed up to the woods and the smell of food would have naturally attracted a hungry dog. My parents drove to the restaurant several consecutive mornings, when it was still cool. No sign of me. About the fourth morning a lady drove up in her vehicle and said she had seen me and called in the sighting. As she described the dog she had spotted, my folks soon realized she had seen a different dog.

Once, when the family was away on vacation to a distant state, they received a call about me. They were glad to receive some news, any news. Problem was they could do nothing from 750 miles away from home.

My picture was posted on a bulletin board at the local animal control/shelter building. Every second or third day dad or mom would drive there to see if I had been captured. Each time they left disheartened. Then one day, a lady called from outside the shelter and said she'd seen one of the employees unloading me from his vehicle into the holding cage area! Naturally, a quick trip was made to the shelter, but once again someone had mistaken another dog for me. Those trips to the shelter were difficult for Mom and Dad. They would see over a hundred dogs, in all different conditions, waiting for a home, for someone, anyone, to adopt them and love them.

In some ways the situation at the animal shelter mirrors the world. People are hoping to be loved unconditionally. They often go to extremes to get others to love them (engaging in activities that they don't enjoy, practices that go against the grain of their consciences and convictions, etc.) not realizing that Someone already does love them unconditionally and has worked to gain their freedom and adopt them into His family. All this, of course, refers to what God has done for all people. He loves us and when we all wandered He went on a search-and-rescue mission. He provided the payment for our sins through His Son, Jesus Christ. He seeks us out, through the Holy Spirit and desires to adopt us into His family. He promises forgiveness of all our sin and to give us life eternal if we will believe His promise to forgive and give life (John 6:47).

There was another way the shelter reflected the world too. It wasn't a pleasant place to go. As you can imagine, with more than 100 dogs and cats doing their "business" inside a building on cement floors, it sure doesn't smell very good. Similarly, to be with lost people in their natural settings will not often be very pleasant. Question is, are you interested in lost people enough to overlook the messes they make, the filth they live in?

Dad says the saddest revelation he had in the two months I was gone on my long journey was that he found he was at times far more interested in the physical well-being of a dog than he was in the spiritual well-being of lost people. I don't know all the ways of God, but that may be the one lesson God wanted to teach him during that season of life.

The bike riding, walking the neighborhood and driving the streets within several miles of home continued for the next several weeks.

Hopes of my return faded but were not completely extinguished. Occasionally a call would come from yet another location in town. The common denominator to all these calls were these: they always involved well meaning, just-trying-to- be-helpful people, a rise of hopes, a fruitless search of another neighborhood or location and yet another disappointment. What was most maddening was the fact that my family could not know for certain if the people were truly seeing me or just a dog who resembled me. They wondered if I was still alive and, if so, was I even in the area? By now with so many weeks having past, if I only had walked a mile per day, I could have been 30-50 miles from home.

A SIGHTING!

In late July, after about two weeks of no sightings, my family decided to attempt one more internet-based attempt to find me. The youngest daughter placed another ad on a local sight, along with a picture and an offer of a reward for my safe return.

About three days after the advertisement was posted, they received a phone call of a sighting. The young couple that called had spotted a dog that fit my description, in their back yard, the night before the call. They called again later to say that the dog was currently in their yard!

Dad and mom drove to the couple's house, about 2 miles away from their house by road, but only about a mile away if you went through the woods, "as the crow flies" as they say. By the time they arrived, there was no dog present. After all the false alarms, Dad and Mom were skeptical of whether or not the couple had actually seen me. The young woman not only described me perfectly but also had had the presence of mind to take a picture on her phone. When she showed them the picture, it was me!

Their hopes skyrocketed. I had been in the same yard twice in recent days. The couple said the first time they had spotted me, they had been grilling out hamburgers and hot dogs in the back yard with some friends. Evidently the smell of the grilling and my hunger drove me out of the woods and into their yard.

SO CLOSE!

Hopes of my safe return reached a new high. The young couple graciously told mom and dad they could come over any time to try to find me in the woods and area near their house. The next night began a routine that would last for some time. Dad and Mom, and occasionally their youngest daughter, would drive the two to three miles to Elvin and Courtney's home to see if they might spot me and catch me. They would set up lawn chairs in the couple's back yard and bring some food along as a treat to entice me to come to them.

The second or third day of this effort, sure enough, I came out of the woods and walked into a wooded section of Elvin and Courtney's back yard. Dad, Mom and Allegra were overjoyed but kept their excitement inside so as not to startle me. They began calling my name, "Oscar…Oscar, come here boy." As they called, dad held out a piece of hot dog as a treat. I was scared and cautious. Since I had been a part of their family for only three months before I got lost, I had only been Oscar for three months, after fifteen months of being Cody, and it had been two months since anyone had called me by this new name. I did not respond to this name, since I didn't recognize it nor remember the people I had only lived with for three months but had not seen for two months.

They kept calling and dad kept tossing pieces of hot dog just a little less far from him, drawing me ever closer to him. I kept eating pieces of hot dog because I was so hungry. Finally I had come to within three feet of dad for yet another bit of hot dog. He considered lunging at me in hopes of grabbing me or my collar but feared if he missed it would frighten me so badly that I might never come back. He decided against the capture attempt and finally, after twenty-four hot dogs I wandered back into the woods. No that is NOT a misprint, it was twenty-four hot dogs (three eight-packs to be exact). Now you can understand why he now sometimes calls me Oscar Mayer.

My family was disappointed but hopeful. Disappointed they had gotten so close to me, sad to see how much weight I had lost and how frightened I was. Yet they were also hopeful. They felt sure my safe capture would occur the next day, or soon.

The next day, when they returned to Elvin and Courtney's home, I was nowhere in sight. The couple and Courtney's mom, Connie, who live with them, had not seen me all day. After calling and waiting for nearly an hour, darkness fell and with it their hopes fell a bit too. They would later joke that the reason I did not come out of the woods that day was because I was too full to move and was not hungry!

Over the next several days all sorts of things were tried. They grilled out to get the aroma of the grill to coax me out of hiding (yes they hauled the grill, charcoal, hot dogs and hamburgers in dad's truck). On another occasion Dad fashioned a makeshift net (dad fashioned it out of an old volleyball net that he cut up into several pieces and laced together) and attached cords to it and rigged it up so that when I walked on the net, he could pull the cords, draped over a tree limb and catch me in the net. I did come out of hiding that day, but the net so frightened me I would not venture out on to it. Yet another method they tried was to put some wire fencing in the back yard with two opening on either end. Each end had wire, fashioned like an accordion door and ropes and when I walked inside the "corral" they would close the front and back with me in the enclosure. I didn't even bother to show up for that idea.

Finally they just gave up on all the methods and asked Elvin and Courtney to keep on trying to coax me into custody. Hopes began to fade a bit as the sightings became a bit sporadic, one every second or third day. About that time Dad and Mom had to take their youngest daughter off to her first year of college, about two hundred miles from home. They would be gone for two days helping her get moved in and unpacked. They knew that they would not be able to catch me in the next two days, even if there was a sighting.

SAFELY HOME!

Dad and Mom arrived home from the trip to their youngest daughter's college around 2:00 PM on a Wednesday. They unpacked, had supper and watched some television. Around 10:30 PM, as they were preparing to get ready to go to bed, mom's cell phone rang. It was Courtney, the young lady whose yard I'd been hanging out in. She told mom that her husband, Elvin, had captured me and that they had a hold of me and a leash on me! Mom and dad got dressed as quickly as possible and dashed over to their house. There I was, frightened, very thin and smelly. Dad gladly paid the reward money that had been offered, scooped my up into his arms and got in the back seat of Mom's SUV. Mom drove us all home and that night dad slept on the couch out in the loft, with me on the floor beside him.

The next day Mom took the day off from work to help me get accustomed to my surroundings. Since the weather was warm, they bathed me outside and gave me a good brushing. Soon after that they took me to the veterinarian. When the vet's office staff weighed me, I tipped the scales at 35 pounds. Only a few months before, during me last visit, I had weighed 55 pounds. In two months of being lost, I had lost nearly 40% of my body weight.

Dad says that would be like a 220 pound man losing weight down to 140 pounds in two months!

Dad and Mom say my coming home gave everyone a reason to celebrate. It was so gracious of God to allow my return to be on the same day that they had left their youngest at college, thus officially becoming "empty nesters". Dad says it reminds him of the story that is commonly called the prodigal son. If you're not familiar with the story, it's found in the Bible, in the gospel of Luke 15:11-32. The story is the third part of a single parable. The parable has one main point, God's love for people, especially those that others consider to be too far gone to be reached and loved. It tells of a shepherd who discovers one of his one hundred sheep is missing and searches for it. The second part tells of a woman with ten coins (probably her dowry) who lost one and searched high and low until she found it. Finally there's the lost son, the prodigal. He's one of two brothers. One thread that ties the story's three parts together is the response of the shepherd, the woman and the father. The shepherd, "Rejoice with me, for I have found my sheep which was lost" (15:6). The woman, "Rejoice with me, for I have found the coin which I had lost" (15:9). Finally the father, speaking to his indignant older son, "But we had to be merry and rejoice, for this brother of yours was dead and has begun to live, and was lost and has been found" (15:32).

The story, with its three parts, was told because many religious leaders did not like who Jesus associated with. He associated with what they considered the untouchables, the pariah of the culture.

He not only associated with them, he befriended and loved them. How the Father celebrates when a wandering son or daughter returns home. He did not scold the son for how long he'd been gone, how much money he'd wasted, only embraced him and ordered the fatted calf to be prepared for a celebration befitting the situation of a lost son's return.

You can be sure, as with the prodigal's return, my dad put on the fatted, calf so to speak. I had lost 40% of my body weight and they were excited to see me. Rather than one meal a day, I was fed twice daily for the first six weeks after my return. I also received extra treats for no good reason other than just being home. I got a new collar and a couple more baths, Mom said I smelled like I'd been sleeping in a dump and eating road kill.

As an aside, the way I was captured was as follows: The young man who captured me, Elvin, is in the military. He put a snare on the ground, sort of like a cowboy's lasso, laying in the grass in his back yard. Inside the circle, the lasso, he put a bowl of food. My hunger drew me harder than my fear repelled me. When I began

to eat, he quickly pulled the snare and it snagged my front left

paw. You could say, in this case, the way to capture a frightened

dog, who has been on the run for two months, is through his

stomach.

EPILOGUE

Well that's my story…. I've had quite an adventuresome life for a three year old dog, haven't I? I have some physical issues with my right front paw and leg. I have some psychological issues (I'm frightened easily and by almost everything). It was out of this fear that I wandered from my back yard that fateful day last year. My two months on the run were by far that worst days of my life, losing nearly 40% of my total body weight.

But it's not all bad, I have a great family that loves me dearly, searched for me frantically, prayed for me fervently and paid dearly for my safe return. Since returning they have been extraordinarily kind. My Dad's dad, "Papa", gives his German shepherd Cheetos at lunch almost every day for a snack, so Dad followed suit. Every now and then he goes to Arby's and gets me and Mollie and Arby's Junior to split. Some would say I have an idyllic life, I wouldn't argue with them. Just wish I could talk dad into letting me have twenty-four hot dogs again someday, like I did that fateful day in the woods last summer. Granny, Dad's mom, is fond of quoting a verse from the biblical book of

Proverbs, "A righteous man has regard for the life of his beast" (12:10). Since that is so, I must say I was adopted into a really good family. I could have been left to sit at The Safe Haven, being passed over by hundreds of people in search of a cute puppy, but graciously Allegra, Mom, and Dad adopted me into their family. My life has never been better.

Thanks for reading my story, I hope in some way it has made you smile, perhaps ponder a bit and maybe even think about God's grace toward you through His Son, Jesus Christ.

"Look at the birds of the air, that they

do not sow, neither do they reap, nor gather

into barns, and yet your heavenly Father

feeds them...."

Matthew 6:26

www.ingramcontent.com/pod-product-compliance
Lightning Source LLC
Chambersburg PA
CBHW081403290426
44110CB00018B/2467